DON'T GET MARRIED IF...

Building a strong marriage that will last forever

Cynthia White Greene

Don't Get Married If...
By Cynthia White Greene

Copyright 2014
Cover Design by: Katie Brady Design
ISBN-13: 978-1503391062
ISBN-10: 150339106X

All rights reserved. The reproduction, transmission or utilization of this work in whole or part in any form by electronic, mechanical or other means, now known or hereafter invented, including xerography, photocopying and recording, or in any information storage or retrieval system is strictly forbidden without written permission by the author.

Dedication

God is my love, my heart, my friend, the very essence of who I am. Without Him, I could do nothing, and I would be nothing. For real! So, I give thanks to Him first.

Second, who can do anything without having the BEST partner on earth! My husband, James, is THE best husband in the entire world, and we KNOW we have the BEST marriage on earth. He is my strongest supporter, my best friend, my travel partner, and adventure seeker. Thank you Honey for being all that you can be so I can be all that I am called to be. With God, we cannot and will not fail! We have FAVOR!

Believing you will be blessed with a marriage beyond your wildest dreams. Stay true to yourself & the journey will be good. Blessings,

Cynthia Greene

Contents

Foreword	7
Prologue	9

Don't Get Married If...

1.	...You are not 100% sure you are making the right decision!..	12
2.	...You're not in love!	14
3.	...You don't know how to share!	16
4.	...You're not ready to give of yourself to your mate 100%!....	18
5.	... You don't know how to communicate!	20
6.	... You don't know how to be a good listener!	22
7.	... You can't be supportive	24
8.	...You're not a team player!	26
9.	...You haven't grown up!	28
10.	...You don't get along!	30
11.	... You argue all the time!	32
12.	...The two of you aren't like-minded!.	34
13.	... You don't have a vision or plan for your marriage (or life)!	36
14.	... You're not prepared spiritually!	38
15.	... You can't be faithful!	40
16.	... You're not best friends!	42
17.	... YOU'RE NOT READY!	44

Epilogue	49
Scripture Index	51
Acknowledgements	53

Foreword

It's no secret that marriages are under major attack in our society. The very definition of the word "marriage" has been challenged on every hand, as it has been put into the hands of our government, as opposed to leaving it in the hands of God and His church. The battle has been steadfast but far from over.

It gives me great joy to know that God is raising up couples, godly men and women, who will not settle for the world's stance on what He has created. Marriage was His first institution, and it is to be protected, valued, and honored as such. James and Cynthia Greene are one of those couples taking a mighty stand. They understand the responsibility they have to be on the forefront of this battle, and I'm so glad they have accepted.

As I read this book, "Don't Get Married If...", I saw so much of what's needed for married couples and singles, alike. This is not a condemnation of the choices one has made in their past or even may feel in their present but rather a growth opportunity that comes in many flavors. I love that the perspective has not been narrowed but broadened by the variety of ideas which help to bring and keep "life" in a marriage covenant.

If you are single, you should have this book. If you are contemplating marriage, this is a keeper. If you're already married and need a little extra "umph", this book will bring you life! Wherever you are, there's always more. In either of these statuses listed, preventive maintenance can make life a much smoother ride. Take the time to invest in you and your relationship. Then, look for the return on your investment!

May your eyes and hearts be open and your spirit ready to receive the beauty of what God has ordained from the beginning of time. You are not only saving yourself, but you may also be saving your legacy!

With God's blessing and His love,

Kashonna Holland
Life Coach, Simply Kashonna

Prologue

The premise of this book is to make people aware that they should search themselves before getting married and make sure they address their own personal issues, and if you're already married, search yourself again. Many people will pick up this book thinking it is for the "unmarried", those who are single, thinking about getting married, or are engaged. This is true, but it can also be for the married.

I know you say, "How can that be?" (based on the title). Well, if we had issues before we got married, then nine times out of ten, we have issues after we are married. We shouldn't ignore the things we bring into a marriage. We have to be willing to make adjustments. And sometimes, adjustments are not easy. For example, if we were "selfish" before we got married, and we're still "selfish", how can we expect to get along with our mate and be everything to them they need us to be? I mean, that is our goal, isn't it?

No one or nothing really teaches or trains us about how to be married. However, we can seek out tools, such as the ones found in books, workshops, counselors, etc. to help us work on some of the things we struggle with. If you think you don't have personal struggles or issues, ask your mate. However, it's best to do your own soul searching. As you browse through this book, let the power of God guide you. Ask Him what you must do to better understand Him, your mate, but most of all, yourself.

In this book, you will find a "Don't Get Married If…" quote, a relevant scripture, my personal comments with nuggets of wisdom, confessions, and a space for you to reflect on your own relationship. I started writing this book back in 2001 or 2002 through a small project I decided to do. The idea came to me from so many people asking for my advice about marriage and relationships. So, I decided to approach people and ask them to complete this statement:

"Don't Get Married If….." Therefore, the quotes in this book are from people just like you and me. It does not by any means encompass every response that I received. There is a scripture for each quote to refer to, for a true answer from the Word of God, and then there is practical advice or suggestions on how a person can deal with these issues.

As I already stated, this book is written for single people, those who are engaged, and those who are thinking about getting married someday. It's about preparing for marriage but also about taking these tools to heart to work on things you may have going on. But if you're already married, use this book as a tool to do a review. Take these tools and use them from a personal self-help perspective. Happy searching!

DON'T GET MARRIED *IF...*

DON'T GET MARRIED *IF*...
...You are not 100% sure you are making the right decision!

A double-minded man is unstable in all his ways.

JAMES 1:8

What's your gut saying? Did you talk to God about it, your family, friends, or pastor? Is your spirit happy about your decision? Then don't let anybody stop you. Go for what you know! Is everyone telling you "Don't do it!"? If that's the case, you know you've seen all the warning signs, so listen to your gut! Search the warning signs you've seen but ignored. Bounce them off of a close friend or relative and really "listen" to what they have to say. Then sleep on it, pray over it, and make a decision if this or they are right for you. If you are straddling the fence then that is surely a sign of double-mindedness and you do not have a clear answer from God.

Confessions:

- I will not ignore the warnings signs in relationships.
- I will not make any major life decisions until I have consulted with God.
- If I have peace about my decision, I will move forward with confidence.

Reflection Point

I know I am making the right decision(s) in my relationship because

_____

_____

_____

_____

I know I may not be making the right decision(s) in my relationship because

_____

_____

_____

_____

DON'T GET MARRIED *IF*...
...You're not in love!

Love is patient and kind. Love is not jealous or boastful or proud or rude. Love does not demand its own way. Love is not irritable, and it keeps no record of when it has been wronged. It is never glad about injustice but rejoices whenever the truth wins out. Love never gives up, never loses faith, is always hopeful, and endures through every circumstance. Love will last forever...

1 Corinthian 13:4-8

They say love is a tricky word. And in love is even trickier. But when a heart loves, it knows nothing and no one can change that. What is your heart saying about this other person you're thinking about marrying? When you get married it's stated that "you're in love." As marriage goes on, many people say, "I love him or her, but I'm not in love." In the Bible, perfect means "mature." Perfect love grows from perfecting or maturing love. Have you perfected love for yourself, for others, and for the one you love? You can't base your marriage on being in love. Base your marriage on that perfect love, maturing, growing love, and you will find eternal love that lasts forever!

Confessions:

- I must love myself first before I can give my love away.
- Marriage requires me to grow in love, not simply be in love.
- Anxiety and fear are not recipes for perfect love.

Reflection Point

I know I love my mate because

_____

_____

_____

_____

I know my mate loves me because

_____

_____

_____

_____

I know I may not be in love with my mate because

_____

_____

_____

_____

I know my mate may not be in love with me because

_____

_____

_____

_____

DON'T GET MARRIED *IF...*
...You don't know how to share!

Freely ye have received, freely give.

MATTHEW 10:8

Is there anything you are not willing to give up for the one you love? Really think about this and know what you can give and cannot give up. Did you grow up sharing with siblings and others? Do you volunteer, serve in the community, give of yourself, your time, or your finances to others? If you do, then you may be more used to giving. If you have never done these things or don't have a desire to, then you may have a problem with sharing.

Can you share with them your credit report, what's in your bank account, access to your cell phone, personal computer, internet, and email accounts? Will you share the last piece of meat on your plate or some of your most private secrets? These are things you really need to think about before you get married or work on if you are married, and you've been having issues about this very topic. Figure out what you can do to change the direction of reaching out beyond yourself.

Confessions:

- I understand that marriage requires sacrifice
- Sometimes that means I put my desires and my needs second.

Reflection Point

I am willing to share everything I have because

_____

_____

_____

_____

I believe my mate is willing to share everything because

_____

_____

_____

_____

DON'T GET MARRIED IF...
...You're not ready to give of yourself to your mate 100%!

The generous prosper and are satisfied; those who refresh others will themselves be refreshed.

Proverbs 11:25

There is a difference between sharing your "stuff" and giving of yourself. Marriage is NOT 50/50. It's 100/100! What part of yourself are you holding back? Are you open, honest? Do you like to cook if he likes home-cooked food? When a disagreement comes, you have to be willing to be there in the moment, proactively listening, willing to work it out, and come to some agreement, even if it means to agree to disagree. You have to give your mate everything you've got. You can't be half-stepping.

Do you even know what your mate needs from you? They may not need you to give them something; they may just want your time and attention. Are you willing to sacrifice your wants for their needs? Believe that if you give of yourself to them, they will give of themselves to you. That's a win-win situation, and you can't lose! What are you willing to sacrifice to make your relationship work?

Confessions:

- I understand that marriage requires sacrifice, and sometimes that means I put my desires and my needs second.
- I am willing to put my pride to the side and give my future mate my all.
- I am confident when I love my mate the right way, I will get the same love in return.

Reflection Point

Giving 100% means I can

_____

_____

_____

_____

My mate giving 100% means they are able to

_____

_____

_____

_____

DON'T GET MARRIED IF...
...You don't know how to communicate!

*A gentle answer turns away wrath,
but a harsh word stirs up anger*

PROVERBS 15:1

Yes! You have to be "willing" to communicate and share your thoughts, ideas, interests and needs. There are all types of communication. Can you communicate with others verbally, non-verbally, and written in a mature and open manner? Are you a good listener? Open communication is the key to understanding what the other person is saying. You have to be present in the moment. Most of us can't read minds! We need to hear what you are saying, understand what you are saying, and be able to communicate about what is being said.

Confessions:

- I will be present with my mate and acknowledge his/her feelings.
- I will not miss an opportunity to communicate and express my desires and needs.

Reflection Point

The way I communicate best is by

___

___

___

___

The way my mate communicates best is by

___

___

___

___

One way we can improve communication is by

___

___

___

___

DON'T GET MARRIED *IF...*
...You don't know how to be a good listener!

Wherefore, my believed brethren, let every man be swift to hear, slow to speak, slow to wrath.

JAMES 1:19

Who gets the last word? Is that important or is making sure you both understand the other's point of view, and you come to a mutual understanding? Listening AND hearing is the key! In order to listen, you have to be silent—slow to speak—and you should try to understand things from the speaker's point of view be "slow to wrath." When sharing what you have to say, make sure the person understands what you are saying. Sometimes, it is best to repeat what was said back to the person and make sure you understood the point they were trying to make. The key is to just be there for each other and be a sounding board they can rely on.

Confessions:

- I will talk less and listen more in my relationship.
- I will be intentional about truly understanding my mate's point of view.
- I will not be dismissive about my mate's feelings or perspective.

Reflection Point

The best time for me to have a good listening session with my mate is when

_____

_____

_____

_____

The best time my mate is willing to listen is when

_____

_____

_____

_____

One thing we will do to improve our listening skills with each other is

_____

_____

_____

_____

DON'T' GET MARRIED *IF...*
...You can't be supportive!

Wherefore comfort yourself together, and edify one another, even as also ye do.

I THESSALONIANS 5:11

Do you believe in her or him? Can you see their vision? Do you support his/her dream even if you don't understand it? Support is powerful and encouraging. Just because you don't agree, doesn't mean it's not right for the other person. Just because you can't see what they see, doesn't mean they don't know what they're talking about. Allow your mate to grow. Be their biggest cheerleader and support them when you can.

Confessions:

- I will not discourage my mate from dreaming big and pursuing his/her goals.
- I will be supportive of his/her endeavors, offer encouragement, and be his/her biggest cheerleader.

Reflection Point

Some of my biggest dreams I would like support from my mate on are

_____
_____
_____
_____

Some of my mate's biggest dreams I would support them on are

_____
_____
_____
_____

DON'T GET MARRIED *IF...*
...You're not a team player!

Behold, how good and pleasant it is for brethren to dwell together in unity.

PSALM 133:1

Once you are married, you are ONE. One in God and one as a team. You gotta have your teammate's back. Do you? We have all heard the saying, "There is no I in team." Every player on the team has a part or a role to play. Take your position. Do whatever it takes to help each other get the job done. These days, there are not many roles which are considered female roles or male roles. Everyone is doing everything to achieve the things that need to get done. Make winning the goal and you will always be on the same team!

Confessions:

- My mate and I make a winning team!
- I will not cause division in my marriage by going it alone.
- My mate and I are better together.

Reflection Point

I will be a great team player with my mate by

_____

_____

_____

_____

My mate can be a great team player to me by

_____

_____

_____

_____

DON'T GET MARRIED *IF...*
...You haven't grown up!

When I was a child, I talked like a child, I thought like a child, I reasoned like a child. When I became a man, I put the ways of childhood behind me.

I Corinthians 13:11

What things from your childhood are you still holding on to? Are you mature in the Word? Are you a mature adult? Putting away childish things can free you into adulthood. What kinds of things describe a child that doesn't fit an adult? Things such as they depend on their parents for food, shelter, and clothing; they throw temper tantrums or cry when they don't get their way; they can't do things for themselves; they can't do the things that an adult should do once they turn 18.

There is another scripture that talks about "leaving your parents and cleaving to your mate." Don't run to mama every time you don't get your way or every time you need something. Work it out together. Trust me when I tell you, you will regret sharing all your business with others because when you make up and move on, forgiving and forgetting, those folks won't.

Confessions:

- I will not allow the negative experiences of the past to spill over into my marriage.
- I commit to work through our marital issues like a mature adult and not involve outsiders, unless I am led to do so.

Reflection Point

Some of the baggage I need to let go of in order to grow up/mature are

_____

_____

_____

_____

Some things my mate needs to do to grow up/mature are

_____

_____

_____

_____

DON'T GET MARRIED *IF...*
...You don't get along!

Can two walk together, except they be agreed?

AMOS 3:3

What types of disagreements do you have? Are they always about the same things? If so, it's time to seek wise counsel. You don't have to agree on everything, every time, but you certainly should be in agreement concerning most things, especially the important things. What discussions have you had about money or finances, about children, about goals for the future, about purchasing a home, about family and friends, about your past? Being open and honest and talking about an issue before it happens can help eliminate issues that come up when discussing certain topics later. Pull out the pen and paper, make a list, and get to sharing about the important stuff!

Confessions:

- I will be intentional about understanding my mate's position on critical aspects of our lives.
- I will commit to asking and answering the tough questions, will not keep secrets, and will work toward resolving any issues which may arise.

Reflection Point

Some of the things we do not agree on are

_____

_____

_____

_____

What I will work on so we can have more agreements is

_____

_____

_____

_____

DON'T GET MARRIED *IF*...
...You argue all the time!

Cease from anger, and forsake wrath:
fret not thyself in any wise to do evil.

PSALM 37:8

Simply said, if you're angry all the time, seek professional help. Nobody wants to be around a surly and mean person. If you're arguing every day or every other day, things are out of whack, and that's not fun. Think about what is making you so angry. Is there anything you can change about yourself, first? Search yourself and figure out what's driving that feeling. Talk to your partner in a neutral setting where you can have a low, quiet conversation. Always be willing to look at yourself and what you may be doing or saying before you point the finger. Seek peace first.

Confessions:

- I will strive to be a peacemaker in my relationship and in my home.
- I do not need to have the last word in a discussion or argument.

Reflection Point

These are the things that push my button and cause me to be angry

_____

_____

_____

_____

These are the things I know that push my mate's button and cause them to be angry

_____

_____

_____

_____

We will do the following so we do not "push" each other's buttons

_____

_____

_____

_____

DON'T GET MARRIED *IF...*
...The two of you aren't like-minded!

Fulfill ye my joy, that ye be likeminded, having the same love, being of one accord, of one mind.

PHILIPPIANS 2:2

Of course this doesn't mean you think alike on everything, but it does mean you have many of the same values and morals. You should definitely be on one accord when it comes to topics such as religion, having or raising children, your future goals, finances, etc. According to the Word, that's how our Father gets joy! He wants us to love the way He loves, be in agreement, and be mindful of the things He is mindful of. He puts us first. Put your mate first, and then you will always be first!

Confessions:

- My mate will share the same spiritual and moral code that I have.
- I will seek to be on one accord with my mate.

Reflection Point

We share the same values about

_____

_____

_____

_____

We do not share the same values when it comes to

_____

_____

_____

_____

We need to discuss the following in order to be more on one accord

_____

_____

_____

_____

DON'T GET MARRIED *IF...*
...You don't have a vision or plan for your marriage (or your life)!

And the Lord answered me and said,
Write the vision, and make it plain upon tables,
that he may run that readeth it.

HABAKKUK 2:2

If you don't have a plan, most likely you will float through life without accomplishing things you would like to. Does your whole future need to be mapped out? Of course not, but every person and every relationship should be on a mission toward something. Write a mission statement for yourself, for your relationship, and then set small goals to accomplish it. The Word says, if you write it, read it, you can run with it, meaning you will not only accomplish it, but it will carry you far. If you don't have a mission, a purpose, a plan, or a goal, then you will probably not run very far from where you started.

Confessions:

- I will pursue and fulfil God's purpose for my life and for my marriage.
- I will write goals for my life and for my marriage, reflect on them, and update them often.

Reflection Point

The vison for my life is

_____

_____

_____

_____

The vision for our marriage is

_____

_____

_____

_____

DON'T GET MARRIED *IF...*
...You're not prepared spiritually!

Put on the whole armor of God, that ye may be able to withstand the wiles of the devil.

EPHESIANS 6:11

First of all, do you have a personal relationship with the Lord? The Word is your weapon. Know it and use it. Secondly, does the person you're with have one? If the answer is not yes, then you're not ready for a true commitment. You have to know how to commit to the Lord before you know how to commit to another person. If you do have a relationship with the Lord, what are you doing to make sure you grow daily? It's not anybody's responsibility to help you grow higher in the Lord but yourself. However, there are other things in place on this earth to help you, such as going to church, reading the Word regularly, spending quality time in prayer and worship, and fellowshipping with like-minded people.

Confessions:

- I will spend time in God's Word regularly as it is the blueprint for my life and for my marriage.
- My mate will have a heart for God and be committed to the things of God.

Reflection Point

I grow spiritually daily by doing the following

_____

_____

_____

_____

My mate grows spiritually daily by doing the following

_____

_____

_____

_____

We grow together spiritually daily by doing the following

_____

_____

_____

_____

DON'T GET MARRIED *IF*...
...You can't be faithful!

For this is the will of God, even your sanctification, that ye should abstain from fornication.

I Thessalonians 4:3

If you are not willing or ready to only be with your mate for the rest of your life, then you are not ready to be married. Marriage is a sacred union and not to be taken lightly. Your mate deserves loyalty and commitment. He/she deserves your faithfulness. No one and nothing should come between you and your mate. Don't let misjudgement or temptation ruin a good thing. What God has joined together, let no man put asunder!

Confessions:

- I am committed to the sanctity of my marriage, period.
- I will not allow thoughts or images to enter my mind which are perverted or unclean that might open the door to infidelity.

Reflection Point

I know I am ready to be faithful to my mate for the rest of my life because

_____

_____

_____

_____

I know my mate is ready to be faithful to me for the rest of his/her life because

_____

_____

_____

_____

The reasons why my mate may not be ready to be faithful forever are

_____

_____

_____

_____

DON'T GET MARRIED *IF...*
...You're not best friends!

A man that hath friends must shew himself friendly: and there is a friend that sticketh closer than a brother.

PROVERBS 18:24

What wouldn't you do for your friend? You share everything with your best friend. You tell everything to your best friend. You experience everything with your best friend. You don't always agree with everything your friend does, but that's your friend, so you go along with it. When your friend hurts your feelings, wrongs you, tells you when you're wrong, you forgive them. Put that emphasis on your mate, and there is nothing you can't share with each other. When your mate is your best friend, nothing and nobody can come between you.

Confessions:

- My mate is my best friend.
- I will not keep things from my mate, harbor unforgiveness, or cause offense to damper our relationship.

"There's nothing wrong with the husband having his friends and the wife having her friends, but that should not keep you from being best friends. Remember the more you do separate the closer you are to separation."

—CARNELL JONES

Reflection Point

My mate is my best friend because

_____

_____

_____

_____

I know I am my mate's best friend because

_____

_____

_____

_____

Some steps we can take to become best friends are

_____

_____

_____

_____

And…..The final, most popular answer!
DON'T GET MARRIED *IF*…
…YOU'RE NOT READY!

Therefore be ye also ready.

MATTHEW 24:44

Watch ye and pray, lest ye enter into temptation.
The spirit truly is ready, but the flesh is weak.

MARK 14:38

Have you gotten your "house" in order? Take a look at your personal self. Take a look at your spiritual self. Take a look at everything in your "world." Examine your finances (your credit report). Do you have a savings, a plan for retirement, or the income you think you should have at this stage of your life? Is your career where you want it to be, on track to get there, or do you have a plan to get there? Take into consideration education, health, personal relationships, your character, and maturity. Are these things where you want them to be, or how will you get it together?

Do they have to be perfect before you marry? Most certainly not, but at the very least, you should have a plan. Take a long, hard look at these areas, make some decisions, plan, set goals, and get prepared. Have your life in order before you decide to share it with another person. Marriage takes work, and it helps to have a game plan. Discuss these things with your partner, brainstorm together, and come up with a game plan. Remember, it takes giving your all to be a winner. Win! Win! Win!

Confessions:

- I will be purposeful about readying my life for my mate by being responsible with my finances, my time, and my decisions.
- I will make an effort to address any baggage or issues from my childhood which might prevent me from being successful in a relationship.

Reflection Point

I know I am ready to have a successful marriage because I have done the following

_____

_____

_____

_____

I know my mate is ready for a successful marriage because she/he has done the following

_____

_____

_____

_____

I know we are ready together because we have done the following

_____

_____

_____

_____

Okay, so, if you do decide to get married anyway in spite of, or you are already married, know that building the right foundation is the key. The foundation that you build on is God. God is love, and your marriage should be built on the love of God. How do we do that? Through the Word of God. There are so many more scriptures in the Bible about marriage, relationships, the husband, the wife, love, communication, and so much more. There is no reason why we can't find an answer for every question under the sky. Although these are biblical principles, they are also very practical and relevant for today.

What things did you discover as you went through this book that you know you must work on? Make a list and decide how you are going to work on them. You will find an index at the end of this book with the scriptures quoted in this book.

Is anyone perfect? Of course not! Can we strive for perfection? Of course we can! In the Bible, the word perfect means mature. The scripture stated earlier, in 1 Corinthians 13:11 says, "When I was a child, I spake as a child, I understood as a child, but when I became a man, I put away childish things." We grow up from children to adults. We learn things along the way, and as we learn these things, we should mature. We cannot remain the same person we were as children. We should no longer base things on what happened to us as children, on what mama did, or what daddy did, or what someone else did to us. You can't say I waited for my teacher to teach me that or I waited for my daddy to show me that or I never learned this or that.

You are an adult now. You can teach yourself anything you want to learn. The question is, "Do you want it bad enough?" The Word says that "I" put it away. So, put it away, and DON'T GET MARRIED UNTIL YOU DO! If you're married, fix it!! And, don't go trying to fix your mate. You work on you, and they can work on themselves. Once you've done a little soul-searching, a little self-examination, and a whole lot of praying and seeking, then you can work on things together. If you really want your marriage to work and work right, you will be willing to put the work in. And, don't think it's a one-time thing. Marriage is work over and over again. It's similar to a job. Although you go to the office everyday and do the same things, you keep showing up every day. Show up in your marriage!

Epilogue

In 2001, I started on a mission. Some of my colleagues asked me to do a workshop on marriage. I didn't feel at the time I was equipped for that. However, because they had so many questions and questions I didn't feel I had all the answers to; I started my very own marriage project. I went up to various people - colleagues, neighbors, friends, family, church family, perfect strangers, and asked them to complete a simple statement. I said to them, "How would you finish this sentence, 'Don't get married if....'?" Most people didn't need time to think about their answer. They just spit it out.

I must admit the most common response was, "If you're not ready." This made me begin to ponder what really makes a couple or a person "ready?" There can be so many answers to that big question because there are so many facets to marriage and relationships. Is there really any one remedy that makes a marriage successful? I don't think so, and although there are many books out there addressing the topic of marriage, I don't believe any of them have one complete answer to this question either.

But can we get on the right track by doing a little research, a little soul-searching, a little counseling, and a little asking the right questions? Sure. Will it make life or our marriage perfect? Certainly not. But, every step helps point you in the right direction to a successful and fulfilling marriage.

I received many different answers from many different people, and I logged them in a small notebook. Over the years, I lost my notes. About ten years later, I ran across the notebook with some of the quotes people had given me and decided it was time to pick back up where I started. I believe everyone can find at least one thing in this book who says, "I might need to work on that." Or, "Maybe I can work on this a little more."

On the other hand, don't feel as if this book is saying, don't get married if you have just one or even ten of these issues. It's not about that. It is simply about awareness and things we should think of, discuss, and perhaps get counseling or advice on, before we decide to take that plunge.

Well, if you've already taken the plunge, guess what? It is never too late to get on track. Do everything, and whatever it takes to have the marriage that you want. It's not rocket science. It's all about being willing to make it work!

Scripture Index

James 1:8

I Corinthians 13:4-8

Matthew 10:8

Proverbs 11:25

Proverbs 15:1

James 1:19

I Thessalonians 5:11

Psalm 133:1

I Corinthians 13:11

Amos 3:3

Psalm 37:8

Philippians 2:2

Habakkuk 2:2

Ephesians 6:11

I Thessalonians 4:3

Proverbs 18:24

Matthew 24:44

Mark 14:38

Acknowledgements

My husband and I have the greatest kids on earth! Kathryn, our little UMD cheerleader, you have bigger things to accomplish than you will ever know at the young age of 19. Your love for animals of every kind will bring you great joy. Go Terps!

Andrew, your dreams are phenomenal! You knew at the age of 14 what you were destined to do. I can't wait to see where God elevates you in the music industry! Do your thing Kydnice! Natasha, you have so much inside of you. Don't ever let your dreams stay on the back shelf. You go after whatever it is you want. Antwine, you have a big heart. You will be blessed for the sacrifice you are making to help the one who has helped you. You will do great things in life. Keep your eyes open for those opportunities that will be thrown your way.

I would like to say thank you to my parents Maretha White Lewis and David E. White. You both raised me well by putting Christ first from the day I was born. My dad always says he has the best kids on earth. Well, since they are my siblings—and I am one of them—I agree. Thank you siblings; Theresa White Cooper (and Lamar), Monee White Jackson (and Corey) and Michael White.

Additionally, my friends are many, but I will mention my lifelong friends from childhood, whom I love dearly, Tracey Veale and Linda Rascoe, my 'Sista's at The Well' group Diane McClean, Darriene Ferres-Merchant, Tonya Malloy, Charmaine Jackson, and Camille Malone. To my Saturday Night Live marriage group, thank you for being the stone that helps keep our marriage foundation strong.

To my previous church family at I5 Church, you helped propel me to my next level before I relocated too far to travel back there every week. Varle Rollins Ministry family and Apostle Varle, the impartations in my life and your heart's cry for this region leaves me in awe! To my new church family, Victory Christian Ministries International and my pastors, Apostles Tony and Cynthia Brazelton, all I can say is WOW! I love where I am fed weekly, and I am so excited about where God is taking the body of Christ!

Much love to our prayer partners—Irvin and Diahanna Hamilton, David and Kashonna Holland, Eric and Belinda Johnson, Bo and Carla Bowens, Art and Mona Lisa Lynch, Dur and Mary Jane Till and Andre and Tiffany Barber.

Lastly, thank you to Terry Harken productions for photography, Graphic Designer Chaka Gale, Stylist Kiana Whittington of Kiana Whittington Beauty, Book cover design by fiverr and editors Monica Almond and Janice Almond of Zion Publishing and Editing. A special shout out to Monica who went above and beyond the call of duty to help make this book happen.

About the Author

Cynthia White Greene is originally from Fayetteville, NC but currently resides in Upper Marlboro, MD. She is married to who she considers the best husband, friend, provider, dad and lover on earth, James. They have four children; Kathryn, Andrew, Natasha, and Antwine. The sanctity of "Marriage" is a passion of the couple's, which led them to start their own company called "Marriage Built 2 Last, LLC." You may follow them on their website, **www.marriagebuilt2last.com**, on Facebook at **#marriagebuilt2last**, and on Twitter at **@marriageb2l**. Look out for Cynthia's next book entitled, *I'se Married Now!* This one will be perfect for newlyweds and the already "wedded!"

The author can be reached at either
www.marriagebuilt2last.com
or
info@marriagebuilt2last.com